Luis Garavito
Hunting The Beast

The Story of a Colombian Serial Killer

Frances J Armstrong

Copyright © 2017.

All rights reserved. No part of this publication may be reproduced, distributed, or transmitted in any form or by any means, including photocopying, recording, or other electronic or mechanical methods, without the prior written permission of the publisher, except in the case of brief quotations embodied in critical reviews and certain other noncommercial uses permitted by copyright law.

This book is intended for informational and entertainment purposes only. The publisher limits all liability arising from this work to the fullest extent of the law.

Table of Contents

Who is Luis Garavito

The Early Years

Type of Victims and His Patterns

The Investigation

The Arrest of The Beast

Legal Factors

The Public's Response

Inside The Mind Of A Killer

   Brains Are Undeveloped?

   Different Classes of Killers

Is it in Their Genes?

   Abuse Excuse…

   Head Injuries?

   A Cure?

   Is There A Pattern?

Who is Luis Garavito

Luis Alfredo Garavito Cubillos was born on the 25th of January in 1957. He is known as 'The Beast' because he raped and murdered at least 140 young people. Based on the maps that he drew while he was in prison, investigators now believe that number could be closer to 300. Garavito was described by the media as "The worst serial murder in the world."

When Garavito was finally captured, he was given the maximum penalty of 30 years in prison in Columbia. However, because he helped the Colombian police locate the bodies and he confessed to the crime, his sentence was reduced to 22 years. It could also be reduced further due to good behavior and cooperation.

The people of Columbia were quite alarmed that Garavito could be released early and felt that he was not receiving adequate punishment for his crimes. At that time there was no way for his penalty to be extended and the legal system was not equipped to deal with the case properly. However, in 2006 it was found that his sentence could be extended. The delayed release was based on the crimes that he had not confessed to and had not yet been charged for.

The oldest of seven boys, Garavito had suffered both emotional and physical abuse at the hands of his father. During his testimony, he stated that he had been sexually abused when he was a child.

Garavito did not just prey on anyone. He attached children that were between the ages of 8 and 16, the most innocent of people. He would rape them, torture them, kill them and then dismember them.

In 1999 Garavito confessed to killing 140 children and was under investigation for murdering another 172. Out of those 172, he was convicted of murdering 138. The other cases are still pending.

After being convicted of the other 138 cases of murder, 1 year 10 months and 22 days were added to his sentence. According to Colombian law, a person could not be imprisoned for over a 30 year period. Since he was helpful to the police when it came to finding the bodies of the children his sentence was reduced by 8 years.

The Early Years

Garavito's father was an alcoholic who sexually, physically, and emotionally abused his children. By the time that Garavito was sixteen years old, he ran away and tried to start a new life. He began working as soon as he got away from his family.

He spent his time traveling in order to keep his job and even though he moved around frequently, he did have a girlfriend. The girlfriend had a young child and it is reported that Garavito got along with the child wonderfully. He was known by his friends to be a kind man but he was easily angered.

Garavito stated that his father had beaten him when he was a child for any reason. There was always fighting in his home growing up and his father would beat his mother. The children had to deal with constant yelling in the home.

He was also sexually abused by two separate neighbors, repeatedly. He was humiliated. Instead of his father sleeping with his mother, he would sleep with Garavito.

Growing up, his father did not allow him to have any girlfriends or to date. He stated that he was either homosexual or bisexual although it seems that he did not know which.

While he did suffer from alcoholism, he did join AA in an attempt to live a normal life.

When Garavito read Adolf Hitler's biography he stated that he felt bad for Hitler. He said that he could identify with Hitler because he wanted to be respected as well.

At just 13 years old, Garavito was raped by two friends of his father. This caused a tremendous amount of emotional turmoil as well as a lot of confusion for the boy. His thoughts and emotions were twisted and messed up.

Some suggest that while it does not justify his actions, some of the events of his childhood could have lead Garavito to commit these horrendous crimes.

Murderers and Childhood Abuse... Could There Be a Link

It was the story of Jack the Ripper that first spark interest in serial murderers and why they murder. Many studies have been done to determine why people kill or kill multiple times and they continue to be done.

What makes a person kill has perplexed researchers over the years. Trying to understand what makes one person a killer and not another, is quite complex.

Childhood abuse has received a lot of attention not just from the media but from researchers as well. This is because so many murderers and serial killers have claimed that they were abused when they were children either by a parent or a guardian.

While it is true that not all murderers were abused when they were children, research has shown that abused does increase the chances of a person committing a serious crime later in life. Studies have also shown that those who are abused as a child have a much higher chance of becoming an abuser. This has led some researchers to believe that the abuse, whether, personal or having witnessed abuse towards another, affected their behavior later in life.

There have been several studies that have focused on child abuse as it related to specific murderers. For example, Ed Gein and John Wayne Gacy were abused when they were children. Those who exhibit psychopathic behaviors are getting a lot of attention from researchers. The researchers are actually looking at the brains of psychopathic killers in order to understand how the disease affects their behavior.

Another study that was done in 2005 focused on categorizing the type of abuse however, it also went a step further. In this study, researchers worked very hard to find credible reports of the abuse that the murderers claimed took place.

They create four different categories which were physical abuse, sexual abuse, psychological abuse, and neglect.

What they found was that childhood abuse was much higher among the murderer population than it was any other population.

35 percent of all murderers suffered from physical abuse when they were children. Another 26 percent suffered from sexual abuse. 50 percent of the murderers suffered from psychological abuse. 18 percent of them had been neglected and only 2 percent and no report of any abuse.

It was also found that it did not matter if the murderer was disorganized, organized, or mixed, the abuse frequency did not change. In other words, one who was more sexually abused did not become more organized or disorganized compared to someone who was more physically abused.

In order to understand what this meant, researchers had to look at the percentage of murderers that had been abused and compare it to the general population. What was found was that the reported child abuse in murderers was six times higher than it was in the general population.

Only 3 percent of the general population was reported to have been sexually abused while 26 percent of murderers were. That means that the murderers were 9 times more likely to have been sexually abused than the rest of the population.

It was also found that 2 percent of the general population reported some type of psychological abuse while 50 percent of the murderers did. Those who were organized murderers were more likely to have suffered from psychological abuse than disorganized murderers were.

In the end, this study showed suggested that when a child is abused, they have a much higher risk of becoming a murderer than if they are not.

Due to the fact that child abuse often is not reported, it is likely that the figures are a bit higher when it comes to the general population. However, the difference would not be large enough to compare to the abuse that murderers were subjected to.

Of course, this is not a way to justify the crimes, simply a way to understand what leads the murderer to kill.

Type of Victims and His Patterns

Most of us know that different serial killers look for different types of victims. For some it is prostitutes. For others, it is women with long blonde hair and just like the rest of the serial killers; Garavito had a specific type of victim that he would attack. He would look for boys that were between 6 years old and 16 years old. (This is the same age range that Garavito was sexually abused by his father.)

He also only targeted boys that were peasants, orphaned, or homeless. When he confessed Garavito told the police that he would befriend the boys before taking them for a long walk. His intent was to ensure that the boys were tired out by the walk.

Once the boys were worn out, he would use nylon rope to tie them up. Later, after they had been sexually abused and often tortured, he would slit their throats and bury them.

When a profiler is looking at a case, they often focus in on the pattern of the serial killer. Often times these patterns actually break the case. When the murders took place, where the murders took place, what the murderer did with the bodies if the murderer was organized. It is these patterns that help us to create the profile of the killer. To truly understand what type of person we are looking for.

Garavito's weapon of choice was a screwdriver. There were also many times that he dismembered the boys. In many cases, the boy's genitals were removed and then placed in their mouths.

All of the victims' bodies had bite marks on them and it was evident that there had been anal penetration. Several bottles of different lubricants were found near the bodies of the victims as well as liquor bottles. The majority of the victims had been tortured for a prolonged period.

In 1999 there were more than 1.5 million displaced Colombians living on the streets. The dirty, hungry, and poorly dressed little children were just something else that the Colombian people had gotten used to seeing.

They would spend their days begging for money, selling newspapers, shining shoes, or selling chewing gum.

It was also not uncommon for children to disappear in the areas where the poor lived. The children usually came from unstable homes and the economic displacement often makes the family even more unstable.

Most of the time no one even noticed that the children were missing. No one ever asked where the children were. It was not like it is in the US when a child does not show up at school and a parent gets a phone call. No one took the time to concern themselves with the whereabouts of these children, not even their own parents.

If it had been children that had come from rich families that had been disappearing, things would have been much different. Then, the police would have been working the case from the first disappearance and it is likely that many lives would have been saved.

However, according to Garavito, he took advantage of the social and economic issues that Colombia was experiencing. Often times, he would tell the children that he was a teacher that he came from a charitable foundation, he was a priest or even a social worker. There were even times that he pretended that he was handicapped in order to gain the sympathy of the children.

Garavito kept a list of all of the children that he had killed; however, he did not list their names. Some of the bodies were so badly decomposed that it was impossible at the time for them to be identified.

When Garavito confessed to the crimes, 40 million people were filled with fear. There is no death penalty in Colombia however, many people wanted Garavito hung. Some reporters even published their own ideas about what should happen to Garavito. One of them stated that he should have been sliced up just as he had sliced up all of those children.

Even though Garavito confessed to a huge amount of abductions and murders, there were still unsolved crimes involving missing children all across Colombia.

It was because of Garavito as well as the unsolved cases that parents were warned not to let their children go out on their own any longer. They were warned right before Halloween that they should not allow their children to go trick-or-treating without being supervised.

Garavito admitted to killing children all across Colombia and even in Ecuador. The majority of the children that were killed, however, were from the area that Garavito had grown up in near Pereira.

The bodies of the children were found in an area that was filled with vegetation which made it difficult to gather all of the remains. When the bodies were finally recovered, a forensic artist would have to be used to reconstruct the faces in order to determine which children had been found.

The Investigation

It was 1992 when young boys between 6 years of age and 16 started disappearing off of the streets of Colombia at a terrifying rate.

The country was in the middle of a civil war that had lasted decades which left many children on the streets, orphaned, or poor.

The children disappeared for years before anyone took any notice. What tipped the police off? Did someone report these children missing? Was someone out there looking for these young boys?

No. The police had begun finding mass graves all across the country. Sadly the criminal justice department did not do anything to follow up on the graves until 1997.

By that point, they began to realize that there was a large number of missing children. The problem was the missing children were not all missing from the same area. In fact, the children were missing from all over the country.

In February of 1998 two children were found lying next to each other, naked, and dead, on a hill. The following day, just a few meters away from where the two children were found, another body was found. All three of the victims had their hands tied with rope and their throats had been cut. The weapon that was used in the murders was found not far from the bodies.

There were many blood stains on the vegetation in the area. It was found that the victim's genitals had been either cut or severed completely.

Upon closer inspection of the bodies, it was found that they were covered in bite marks and there was evidence of anal penetration. A bottle of lubricant was found at the scene as well. DNA analysis of the DNA that was collected was not performed due to the cost.

At that time, there were several serial killers living in Columbia. It was unknown if these children were the victim of Pedro Lopez who had murdered around 70 children at that time or if there was another murderer on the loose.

Pedro was known for killing only girls. The boys did not fit his MO. It was unlikely that he had changed his pattern and more likely that there was a new killer on the loose. A profile was not done due to funding issues.

There was a piece of paper located at the crime scene which had an address written on it. The paper led to the police to Garavoito's girlfriend at the time.

It was later found that the boys had lived in a nearby town. The boys were 11 years old and 13 years old. They had been friends and worked together on the streets selling gum and fruit to help their families.

One of the boy's mothers told the police that her son had returned home briefly on the day that he had gone missing. He had told his mother that he was going to help a man transport cattle.

It was also noted during the investigation that all of the children seemed to disappear at about 10 in the morning.

Later it was discovered that Garavito would target a boy and then provide them with a gift such as a cake at a local shop. While the boy was eating he would determine if the boy was right. He wanted to make sure that the boy's skin was not too dark, that he was trusting, and so forth.

Once Garavito determined that the boy was right, he would ask them to go for a walk with him or to help him carry something.

Not only did he change his costume on a regular basis but he also changed what he asked of the boys.

For example, he asked for help carrying oranges, harvesting sugar cane, or helping with cattle as well as many other tasks.

He would promise drugs to children who were addicted to them as well. In the beginning, Garavito had started with just offering the children money but the children were suspicious of him. This is why he switched up what he was offering. He decided that he would offer something of just a bit more value than a child would earn on a normal day.

The child would think that they would be able to put some of the money back because their parents would not know and would go with him. No matter what he did, his intent was to lure the child away so that they were unable to return to their home before he assaulted them.

At 6 in the morning on the day after Halloween which is known as The Evening of the Children, Garavito found a victim and offered to help the child collect all of the sweets that had been lost the night before.

Once the bodies of the three boys were found an investigation was opened and investigators started looking for homicide cases all across Colombia that was similar. There had been hundreds of cases that had been reported but many of the children had not been identified and many of the reports did not contain a description of the injuries.

At that time, it was almost impossible to identify a child with dental X-rays or medical reports because the majority of children had not seen a dentist or a doctor. Even to this day, there are 27 known victims who have never been identified.

Facial reconstruction was used in a couple of cases, however, not many of them.

There was in 1995 another series of attacks. This time the children were between the ages of 8 and 10. All of the children had been described as less than intelligent, they came from poor families, and they all disappeared just before noon.

Once again the bodies were found on a hill where the vegetation was thick and not far from town. Evidence suggested that the children were all killed in the same area but not at the same time. The murders took place days apart from one another.

Garavito did not bury the bodies but instead, he left them lying on the side of the hill. It was evident that once Garavito found an area that was suitable for the assaults he would use it multiple times.

Of course, the children would have known that they were in danger once they arrived and saw the bodies and blood; however, they were tied up immediately upon arrival.

Garavito was unable to stop himself even when the situation was dangerous. On the 8th of June in 1996, a young boy was missing from Boyaca. The boy had followed Garavito while riding his own bike. There was no abduction or violence at that point. However, the boy's body was found just five days later.

The boy's mother had immediately began searching for her son and learned that he had been seen with a stranger at the local shop. The stranger, later identified as Garavito had bought the boy as well as a few others sweets. However, the man had left alone.

Just 4 days later Garavito would kill a boy in the town of Pereira which was nearby.

Besides all of the behavior that has already been mentioned, Garavito also decapitated some of his victims or at least tried to do so.

When many of the bodies were found, there was no soft tissue left to identify where any cuts were made. Therefore, the fourth vertebra in the neck had to be checked for notches caused by the knife which was used to slit their throat.

It was determined by these notches that the blade which was used was old and not smooth. Most of the time, Garavito would leave the internal organs in place. He did stab the boys in the abdomen multiple times however; he made no cuts to remove their organs.

There was, however, the exception of one boy that was 10 years old. The boy was killed in January of 1997. The boy was found in a similar situation as the other boys that had been found, however, this time the wounds were not caused by a knife. Instead, they were impaling wounds.

The corpses were only dismembered if they had to be transported out of a house, where a couple of the killings did take place. There were also a few instances when Garavito would place the bodies in plastic bags and use stones to sink them in the local bodies of water.

At most of the crime scenes, empty bottles of cheap schnapps were found. Garavito was an alcoholic and had at one point attended AA meetings in order to try to stop drinking. However, the attempt failed.

He had no problem leaving the empty bottles in plain sight just as he had the dead bodies of the children he had killed.

At this point, it was understood that Garavito knew which would be his killing places and that had divided those killing places up into sectors. Garavito would kill 1 boy per each sector Most of the time Garavito took his time torturing the boys who were most often tied up, however, still able to walk.

The boys were so exhausted however; they were unable to escape due to not being able to run too far too fast. It was evident in all of the cases that anal penetration had taken place however; it is unknown if this happened before or after the boys were murdered.

Most of the children were taken on or close to the weekend which was when they usually spent their time near the marketplace. Garavito lured the boys away during the day because he knew that offering them odd jobs as well as dinner would not raise suspicion.

Before Garavito confessed, no one wanted to accept that one person was responsible for all of the deaths. Because of this even though there was no signs or evidence to prove, people believed that it was Satanists or some secret organization that had killed the children. Some believed that the children had been sacrificed.

This was highly unlikely because none of the murders took place during the same time. The pattern of the killings was very irregular as well.

Some also suggested that the boys had been killed so that their organs could be sold on the black market. However, it was obvious that the crime scenes were very unsterile, and most of the time, the organs still remained in the bodies. Therefore the theory that the boys were killed for organs was dismissed very quickly.

Garavito had previously been arrested under a different name. At that time, there was no fingerprinting done due to the civil war as well as technical problems. By March of 1999, the police had begun checking phone numbers that were found in the clothing of prisoners. Upon checking one specific number it was found that the inmate was not the person he had claimed to be but Garavito.

By this point in the investigation, Garavito was on the list of suspects; however, that list was quite long. It was not long before one of his relatives brought a box to the police that Garavito had brought to her.

In the box, the police found cryptic notes as well as photographs that had been cut out of passports of some of the children that had been murdered. It is not unusual for a murderer to keep trophies from their victims and to Garavito, these pictures were trophies.

There was also a calendar found in the box that had cryptic notes written on it. Later it was found out that Garavito had listed the names of each of his victims on the different dates that he had murdered them. It is still not understood why he made these notes because he was able to easily recall all of the details from every murder as well as the dates that he committed them on.

It was then on the 28th of October in 1999 that Garavito was informed that the police knew who he was and that they had found the evidence of his murders. He was taken in for questioning. While he was being questioned, he quickly confessed to the crimes that he had committed and ask for God as well as mankind to forgive him.

The Arrest of The Beast

On the 22nd of April in 1999, the police arrested Garavito on separate attempted rape charges. During his questioning, he was asked about the murders of the boys as well as the attempted rape.

At the time, the police believed that he was planning on killing the boy that he was attempting to rape and that he would have if a passerby had not saved the boy.

The interrogation was short however; the policed believed that Garavito was The Beast which was what name was given to the murderer before it was known that it was Garavito.

During this interview, Garavito insisted that he was innocent. When the police provided him with a detailed description of the murders, he began crying.

Garavito suffered from a very rare eye condition which meant that he had to have a special type of glasses that were designed specifically for this eye condition.

There was a pair of glasses found at one of the crime scenes which had been designed for that specific condition. Of course, there were usually liquor bottles all around the crime scenes, often times he would leave his underwear or his shoes, and there had been DNA found inside the bodies of many of the boys as well as other items.

At the jail where Garavito was being held, the police scheduled an eye exam for every inmate. It was this eye exam that would link the glasses found at the crime scene to Garavito. Of course, the police were smart and made the eye exam mandatory for every inmate in order to ensure that Garavito did not become suspicious. It also ensured that Garavito did not try to lie while taking the exam.

While Garavito was taking the eye exam, the detectives went into his cell and took DNA samples from the cell, specifically from his pillow.

The DNA was found to match the DNA that the police had found at the crime scenes.

Upon questioning about the murders, Garavito confessed to killing 140 boys and was later charged with killing a total of 172. He was found guilty of killing 138 boys while the police continued to investigate the disappearance of another 172 boys throughout the entire country.

At this point, many people would think that Garavito would spend the rest of his life in prison because if you multiply the maximum murder sentence by the 138 convictions you would get over 1853 years. However, the problem is that in Colombia a person is not allowed to be held in prison for more than 40 continuous years.

Since Garavito helped the police by telling them where the bodies of the boys were, he had his sentence reduced and would only serve 22 years.

Legal Factors

In Colombia, it is very difficult to get different agencies to cooperate with each other due to the constant political issues, the organizational issues, as well as the extreme amount of violence most often due to the paramilitary and guerrilla units.

Compared to more industrialized countries, in Colombia pedophilia is very widespread. This is because the juveniles or the children must earn some type of income. Statistics show that about 40 percent of the children in Columbia live in poverty which means at least 40 percent of the children may be on the street working at any given time. To a pedophile, this is nothing more than a sea of victims to choose from.

Because there are so many children on the street, many of the fall victim to pedophiles. However, it is impossible to prevent the children from being on the street. On top of that, it was very easy for Garavito to just pick up and leave. There were several times that he suddenly left and went to Ecuador.

The public prosecutors or district attorneys have their own investigation units. These units are different from the police and are allowed to conduct investigations all across the country whereas the police can only investigate locally.

In the case of Garavito, the public prosecutors were used as well as a local investigation unit from Armenia, in order to investigate similar crimes across the entire country of Colombia. The Armenian police were used because this was where Garavito was from. On top of that many of the bodies had been located near Armenia. As it turned out, the other investigation units did not share the information that they had collected with the police in Armenia, at least not all of the information.

To this day, the case is actually not closed. During the trial, it was found that Garavito is sane, meaning that he had at least some sense of responsibility for the crimes he committed. This meant that sending him to live in a psychiatric unit for an undefined length of time was out of the question. Therefore he was sentenced to serve his time for his crimes in prison.

Garavito never did make a court appearance. This is because in Colombia when a defendant offers a full confession, there is proof that he committed the crimes, and the evidence backs up the confession, no formal trial is needed.

On top of this, the public was outraged with what Garavito had done and that he had not been stopped sooner. Neither party wanted to go through a trial.

Once in prison, many believed that Garavito would be killed as soon as he was introduced to the general population, therefore, he was kept separate from them.

Garavito lives in fear of being poisoned and will only drink or eat anything if a few specific people give it to him. He and his guards get along well, which only goes to show that he is relaxed in prison and not shy.

When most people who have studied murderers look at Garavito and his case, they find that it is contradictory to the typical intelligent serial killer in several different ways.

Garavito was able to commit so many murders without being detected because he was able to socially adapt. He knew to change his clothing, his character, and what he told the children he needed help with. However, he was unable to change his glasses.

If we look at this alone, it would seem that Garavito was very intelligent or that he had been trained to behave this way. The only thing that he was never able to change was the glasses that he wore. The frames on the glasses were red plastic.

However, when we look at the high number of victims we also have to understand that he was only able to murder this many because of the chaotic atmosphere in Colombia. He was able to blend in around the marketplace, pretending to sell fruit or other items.

He also knew that because the children were living in poverty, the prospect of a job would attract plenty of children.

He was smart enough to take advantage of a situation that was out of everyone's control and he knew that in doing so he would be able to avoid being caught.

He also knew that he had to make sure that the boys were tired out before he attacked them. He knew that if they were not, they would be able to return to town and tell about what he had done. This shows us that he knew what he was doing was wrong and that he would be punished for it if he was caught.

Then there is the other side of him. He is unable to stay on topic when he is talking to someone. His conversation just like his thoughts jumped from one topic to the next. Even if he begins a conversation where he is talking about something he is interested in, it is only a few minutes or even a matter of seconds before he changes the topic.

Because Garavito was never treated by a psychologist in order to deal with the effects of the abuse that he suffered as a child, he is not used to talking about personal topics to other people. Even when he knows it would benefit him.

One example of this happening is when he was speaking about how he had found an article that discussed how a child could deal with being abused. He stated that he had written down notes next to the article and that he found it very interesting.

However, when he was asked why he thought the article grabbed his interest, he immediately changed the topic and pretended as if he had not even heard the question at all. This is very important to understand because we already know that he was abused when he was a child, yet even to this day, he is unable to face the abuse, even after inflicting abuse on so many others.

This leads us to a question. Why do those who are abused end up abusing? It would seem that when a person is abused as a child or at any point in life, they would understand how painful it can be. It would also seem that they would not want anyone else to go through that same pain. So how is it possible that these are the people who often turn into abusers themselves?

I believe that there are a few reasons that those who are abused often turn into abusers. The first reason is that most often when a child is abused by a parent, they tell themselves that they deserved whatever happened to them. The first thing that a child will do is to make the behavior of the parent their fault.

The child believes that they are bad. This leads to confusion in the child but they would rather believe that they are bad, than their parent is bad.

During the abuse, the child feels as if they are completely alone. They have no one in the world to turn to and no place that is safe for them to go. They also often grow up with no guidance and suffer from more than one type of abuse. For example, if a child is physically abused, they are often neglected. A child who is sexually abused may also have to deal with psychological abuse as well.

Life for the child becomes hopeless. They never have the hope that if they are a better person, life will get better. They will also tell themselves that their parent is abusing them because they love them and they are trying to help them learn to do better.

So the number 1 reason is that children who are abused often internalize the abuse, blaming themselves for it.

When a child who is abused grows up and becomes an abuser it is often because they have learned that if they are the biggest meanest bully, they are going to get what they want. They do not learn not to abuse others from being abused. What they learn is that the big bully gets what they want and because of that, the child learns how to bully others.

This is something that many people need to understand when it comes to childhood bullies as well. Most often the child is not a bad child; they are, however, simply displaying behavior that they have seen at home.

This is the second reason that many abused children turn into abusive adults.

The third reason is that the child has never been given the chance to learn empathy. They are not able to put themselves in the position of the person that they are abusing. There is actually evidence that shows that due to childhood trauma, the children did not psychologically develop properly.

Why is this important to understand? It is important for us to understand this because while we may look at an abuser as an evil or sadistic person, it is important for us to remember that they were probably abused themselves.

It is vital for us to recognize this because it shows that even in this day when there are so many resources available; children are still not getting the help that they need after they suffer from abuse.

Later Garavito was given a picture test, (in 2005) which he was unable to understand and he was also unable to solve simple quizzes.

Looking at this from a criminalist standpoint, it is quite remarkable that Garavito was so careful when it came to abducting the boys and yet he still took the photographs out of their ID's as trophies.

It is also odd that Garavito loved to have his picture taken. He had several pictures taken of him working as a street vendor as well as inside of his apartment and many others times as well as places.

In an economy that is challenged, it is not uncommon for people to have to travel for work. Therefore, the fact that Garavito traveled for work was not something that would raise any red flags.

He would live with women who were his own age or even a bit older. Some of the women even had children. Oddly enough according to his girlfriends, Garavito seemed to be a loving father figure to the children. They never claimed that he had abused the children or showed any type of concern about him being near their children.

Many of them told investigators that he loved to play with the children. In one of the cases, Garavito sent money to one of the girlfriends while he was traveling to help take care of the child. It is believed that Garavito did not have any sexual relations with these women however; this is not something that was fully investigated.

The next stereotype about intelligent criminals is that they are controlling and for Garavito at least, this was true. Garavito would try to reach his goals or to get what he wanted by using the most socially accepted methods.

For example, when he wanted his freedom he offered to help the police find the bodies of the victims. He took control of the situation, claiming that he felt sorry for his victims. He also stated that he felt sorry for the children when they would tell him about the abuse they were suffering at home.

However, that did not stop him from torturing them to death.

Garavito also made ambiguous comments about the personal safety of those that he was talking to. Once during an interview with investigators, he told them that they needed to be careful when they were walking the streets alone. It is known that walking the streets alone in Colombia can be very dangerous.

However, investigators found themselves wondering if he had warned them of the danger because he was genuinely concerned about their safety or if he was trying to find out if the investigators were afraid of walking alone, or if he was trying to put himself into a position where he would feel power over the investigators.

The problem that Garavito struggles with when he is trying to take control of a situation is that he did not understand how other people are going to react or what their intentions are.

For example, we all know that Garavito confessed to the crimes and helped the police in order to ensure that he got the shortest sentence possible. However, he did not understand that the police and the investigators were not going to let him simply walk out of prison and back into society.

When he is visited by reporters he often complains that they do not bring him expensive gifts but instead, they bring him items such as t-shirts with their logo on it.

Once, he became so angry that he did not receive an expensive gift that he wrote a letter to the police as if he were an informant. He told the police that he remembered exactly what the reporters looked like as well as what they had talked about.

He behaves like a spoiled brat would when they do not get their way. He literally told on reporters because they did not give him what he wanted.

Then there is the side of Garavito that wants to understand why he does the things that he does. Because Garavito will not speak about his personal life, researchers began speaking with him about other cases.

They asked him what he thought about the different cases. Garavito was very interested in learning about the different cases and always wanted to know how many victims each had. However, even though he was very interested, he was unable to focus on the conversation and soon began talking about a different topic.

When a person meets Garavito they are often given the impression that he is open and friendly. However, there are times, mostly when the conversation gets a little too personal that Garavito will become tense.

He has said that when he is released, he is not going to continue with the murders. He stated that he has gotten everything in his mind sorted out.

Today, Garavito is considered a model prisoner and he will be up for release in 2021. That is just 4 years from the date of this writing.

However, according to the Colombian law, anyone who commits a crime against a child does not receive the benefit of justice. While this does need some clarification, this could mean that Garavito will spend no less than 60 years in prison or that he could spend 80 years in prison. Both cases would ensure that he would die before ever seeing his freedom.

The Public's Response

The people of Columbia were very angry about the fact that Garavito was scheduled for early release. They feel that the punishment does not fit the crimes committed.

Many people have demanded that he serve life in prison or that he receive the death penalty. However, life in prison and the death penalty do not exist in Columbia.

There is no provision in Colombian law or method which would allow for a longer sentence than what Garavito was given. This has shown the people in Colombia that the law was deficient. Since that time the maximum penalty was raised to 60 years.

During an interview with TV host, Pirry, on the 11th of June in 2006, Garavito stated that he wanted to work in politics after he was released from prison in order to help children who had been abused. He worked very hard to minimize what he had done.

Inside The Mind Of A Killer

It has been said that not every psychopath turns into a serial killer but every serial killer is a psychopath. Is this just another saying or is it possible that this is actually true?

According to what the FBI has found while studying both psychopaths and serial killers, there is a link however, it is not a concrete as many people believe.

Of course, not all psychopaths become murderers, however, many serial killers do possess at least a few of the traits that are consistent with a psychopath.

The FBI defines a psychopath as someone who lacks remorse, who is impulsive and who lacks empathy among many other characteristics.

The fact is that there are psychopaths everywhere. We pass them in our everyday lives and know nothing about it. Studies have shown that often times, CEOs, lawyers, and even doctors are psychopaths. These people are much focused, they are driven and they have very little remorse for whatever actions they have to take in order to reach success.

However, it is very rare that these people commit murder or multiple murders. Some people have actually argued that all of us have a few psychopathic tendencies. While this might seem a bit extreme, there are all times that we are driven or that we are impulsive, however, those characteristics do not define who we are.

This simply proves that not all psychopaths are killers. Therefore, you can rest easy knowing that you can go visit your doctor or your lawyer and you will leave their office in one piece. (most of the time)

However, if you are going around killing people and you continue to do so over an extended period of time, do not that show that somewhere in there is a psychopath?

The definition of psychopathy is very broad so it is very difficult for one to compare two people and say that one is a psychopath and the other is not.

For example, Herbert Mullin claimed that he killed 13 people claiming that the voices had told him to do so in order to save the state of California. He had been diagnosed with schizophrenia years before he committed the crimes. Therefore, it was known that he was psychotic however; he was not considered a psychopath.

The statistics actually show that the more gruesome murders are most often committed by those that are psychotics and not those that are psychopaths.

What is the difference between the two? A psychotic has lost his or her connection with reality whereas a psychopath knows that they are committing a crime.

Psychopathy is not considered a mental illness; therefore, it cannot be used in court for a plea of insanity.

Brains Are Undeveloped?

Joanna Dennehy was a mother of two beautiful children when in March of 2013, she murdered three men then she dumped their bodies. Just a couple of days after she killed the three men, she stabbed another in plain sight in the middle of the day.

Only nine minutes after the stabbing, she attacked and stabbed another man then ran away with the man's dog.

During her trial, she had laughed at the crimes she had committed. Of course, she was not the first to do so. Jeffrey Dahmer had stated that if he was given the chance, he would have kept killing. Israel Keyes admitted to killing at least 11 people, however, during his interview, he was telling jokes.

One of the most common things that investigators have noticed when they are interviewing serial killers is that they have no remorse at all.

Adrian Raine who is a professor at the University of Pennsylvania believes that the reason serial killers react this way is because their brains are underdeveloped.

He believes this because after studying the brains of serial killers, he found that they seem to be lacking in the dorsolateral cortex as well as the ventromedial cortex.

The ventromedial cortex helps us with making decisions and it was found that the majority of serial killers have reduced function in this area. The dorsolateral cortex is what allows us to learn from our mistakes. It was shown that the criminals who committed crimes of impulse instead of premeditation lacked functioning in this area.

Since psychopathy is not considered a mental illness, the professor believes that the people who suffer from this disorder should be treated the same as a person who is suffering from another mental illness.

According to a researcher from the UK by the name of Graeme Fairchild, Raine is correct. Fairchild stated that we need to ask ourselves if the psychopath is really responsible for their behavior or if it is due to their underdeveloped brain.

The "Normal" Person Turns Killer?

Imagine being 15 years old and finding out that your dad was a serial killer. Now imagine that this was not a man that had abandoned you before you were born or a man that had nothing to do with you. Imagine that this was the man who took you to school every morning, who helped you with your homework, who told you jokes, and who tucked you into your bed at night.

This is exactly what happened to Melissa Moore. Her father was The Happy Face Killer, Keith Jesperson.

Over a five year period starting in 1990, Jesperson raped and killed 8 women. Most of his victims were prostitutes. This means that when his little girl was just 10 years old, he began committing murder.

Jesperson was a truck driver, so he was gone for long periods of time; however, he always made sure that he had time for his kids. Even after he was convicted his daughter stated that she remembered him as a kind man, a good dad.

This is enough to make any person question if Jesperson was just good at what he did if he was really good at covering his tracks, if there were signs that his family chose to ignore, or if he was just the average man that one day decided to start committing murder.

According to his family, after they found out that he was a serial killer, there were some things that they had overlooked.... His dark side.

His family stated that he would often torture casts that were found wandering around their farm. He told them one time that he knew how he could kill someone and not get caught. One time before he had committed the very last murder, his daughter was riding with him in his truck.

She found a roll of duct tape as well as a pack of cigarettes, however, Jesperson did not smoke that she knew of.

Today he is serving a life sentence for his crimes. His family spent years trying to understand how he was able to be such a loving father while committing these terrible crimes. Finally, Jesperson's father came to the family after he had visited his son and told them that Jesperson had admitted that he had often thought about killing the kids. That was all his family needed to finally let him go.

Different Classes of Killers

There are many different types of killers and over the years they have been classified into categories. This allows us to understand what killer murdered what person and what their reasoning was.

There are visionary killers who claim to hear voices or have psychotic breaks. These are the killers that claim God made them do it or that the voices told them to kill for whatever reason.

Then there are the mission-oriented killers that have for some reason come to the conclusion that it is up to them to rid the world of specific people such as people of a specific race or prostitutes for example. Hitler would be considered a mission-oriented killer as he felt it was his duty to rid the world of the Jewish people.

The third classification is Hedonistic killers which is where the majority of serial killers are categorized. There are subcategories of this specific category which include, lust killers, thrill killers, and comfort killers.

A comfort killer is a person who looks at the murders as nothing more than a speed bump. They believe it is unfortunate but the person got in their way. These types of people do not enjoy killing but they need to get the person out of the way so that they can get a promotion, a job, a girl, or whatever else they are after.

A person that is a lust killer will kill for sexual gratification. Often times they are unable to enjoy sex without violence, however, there are also those that find that the violence increases the sexual gratification. The second type of people if not stopped will eventually be able to enjoy sex at all without being violent.

The thrill killers are the killers that murder people simply because they enjoy killing. These types of people may stalk their target for weeks in advance. They get pleasure from planning out every detail of the murder as well as the execution of the plan.

When we think about a thrill killer, The Zodiac Killer would be a perfect example because even in his letters, he stated that he liked killing because it was fun.

Is it in Their Genes?

According to a professor at the Karolinska Institute in Sweden, killing could be in our genes.

Jari Tiihonen took a blood sample from almost 800 criminals that were incarcerated and performed DNA testing on the blood.

According to the professor, he found that there was a genetic mutation that was found only in violent offenders.

The MAOA gene helps with the production of dopamine which has been linked to aggression. This gene is also called the warrior gene. According to this study, it was found that those who had this warrior gene committed violent crimes 13 times more than those who did not have the gene.

There was also a separate study done in the United States and the researchers found Tilihonen's conclusion to be correct.

This could also explain why the majority of serial killers turn out to be men. The MAOA is only located in the X chromosome. Men are born with only one X chromosome while women are born with 2. This means that while a woman may have this warrior gene it is very likely that they have one normal gene as well, which will almost counteract this warrior gene. However, men will only have the one gene.

OF course, it may be possible that this warrior gene is to blame for some of the murders, however, what happens when things hit a bit closer to home.

According to reports Jeffery Dahmer's father reported suffering from violent fantasies and urges although he never acted on them. Then there is Jesperson's great uncle who was known for sexual sadism, had been committed to a mental hospital, and who killed himself. The way that he killed himself was quite horrific. He drove a nail into his own skull.

Was there something that happened in Jesperson's life which pushed him over the edge causing him to commit murder while his Uncle just suffered from the crazies?

According to James Fallon, a neuroscientist, this could be the case. Oddly enough, however, his test subject was not a murderer but it was himself.

He is not a psychopath, nor is he violent; however, he is quite interested in the brains of serial killers. He has no problem admitting that he is quite obsessed with the topic.

While the doctor has always thought that this is nothing more than curiosity, he found that this obsession is much more than that.

You see, it began when his mother told him that he might want to start researching his own lineage because as she put it, there could be some crazies back there.

Fallon began digging and was startled by what he found. His great-grandfather, Thomas Cornell had in 1667 been executed for killing his mother.

Seven of the descendants of Thomas Cornell ended up in the middle of murders, one of them the famous Lizzie Bordon. Murderers were sprouting up all over his family tree.

That was when Fallon decided to take a scan of his brain. What he found was that his brain was just like the brains of those he had been studying for years, serial killers. What startled him the most was that there was very little activity in the prefrontal cortex, which is the area of the brain that is linked to impulse control as well as ethical behavior.

This is one of the defining marks of someone that is a psychopath. Fallon, the man who was obsessed with studying serial killers suddenly realized he fit the profile perfectly.

What made other people commit murder and not Fallon? Fallon believes that it is because he had parents that cared about him and that he had a pleasant childhood. This is something that most serial killers do not have.

However, had things gone differently, had one person abused him as he was growing up, he may have found himself sitting behind bars instead of studying those that are.

Abuse Excuse...

Fallon believed that he dodged a bullet because he was not abused as a child. He believes that if he had been, he may have ended up being the next murderer in a long line of murderers in his family.

Recently it seems that it is acceptable to blame what happened when a person was a child for the mistakes they make in life. It has become an excuse to use so that the person does not have to take responsibility for their actions.

Sure, the serial killer may have been beaten as a child. Maybe that spree killer suffered from head trauma when they were very young.

Perhaps that pedophile was raised in a home where pedophilia existed. These are all common backgrounds when it comes to murderers and serial killers.

I am not contesting the fact that childhood abuse plays a huge role in the development of the person as they grow up. However, does this mean that being abused as a child is a valid excuse for becoming a serial killer?

You see, for a murderer who claims that they were damaged to the point of committing murder because they were beaten as a child, I can show you a thousand people who were beaten as a child and committed no such crime.

This excuse due to abuse is very dangerous because it does not force the person to take responsibility for their actions. It could also mean that the courts to hold the person responsible for their actions very soon because after all, it was not their fault that they had a hard childhood.

Head Injuries?

I grew up in the 80's I have suffered multiple head injuries because back in those days, helmets were not something that parents worried much about. Heck, they didn't even worry if we were buckled into the car as they were driving 70 miles an hour down the freeway.

But according to a study that was done by Dr. Lewis in 1986, head injuries just might be why murderers murder.

Dr. Lewis studies 15 inmates that were on death row for murder. What she found was that all 15 of the murderers had suffered from some form of head injury when they were children.

Most of the time, the murderers did not even remember that they had been injured and had no idea where their scars had come from.

Dr. Lewis ended up having to look into the medical records of the murderers to find out what had happened to them.

In a separate study, Dr. Lewis looked at 14 juveniles who had committed murder and were on death row. Once again she found that all 14 had some sort of brain injury that resulted in damage when they were a child.

Most psychologists have been critical of the studies because they were performed with such small groups of people and there were no controls. However, we all have to admit that what she found is a bit compelling.

However, this just raises more questions. If the serial killer kills because they have suffered from a brain injury early on in life, is it possible that it is not their fault that they murder? Is it their fault that they are unable to control themselves? Are the murders nothing more than a symptom of a brain injury? If this is, in fact, true, is there a way to treat the brain injury?

A Cure?

There is a theory out there that we cannot hold killers accountable for the murders that they have committed because it is caused by circumstances out of their control. One example of this would be a head injury.

If the murders are nothing more than a symptom of a deeper issue, then we have to ask ourselves if there is a cure for the problem.

Most people would say that there is not a cure for murder especially when it comes to psychopathic serial killers.

According to Dr. Nigel Blackwood who is a forensic psychologist, there is never going to be a cure for those that suffer from psychopathy because a psychopath does not fear being punished in the same way that a normal person does. This tends to make it very hard for a psychopath to be treated while they are in prison.

Most of the time a psychopath can be managed. Dennis Rader who is a psychopath and has been in prison since 2005 has shown nothing but good behavior.

It was found that when a reward system was used for good behavior, Rader thrived in prison. He began looking forward to the small rewards that he would receive for good behavior.

This may show that the reason that he committed the crimes was because he was reward-oriented.

It was 2003 when Darian Rawson stood at the end of the aisle watching his bride to be Kerri walk toward him. Her father held her arm until he gave her away.

That man that gave his daughter way that day was the president of the church council as well as a respected scout leader.

Just two years after her father walked her down the aisle, the FBI would show up to her to her door to inform her that he was the BTK killer.

No one would have suspected that Dennis would have killed 10 people over a 31 year period. During that time, he had also stalked multiple women, killed 2 young boys, and he defiled his victim's bodies.

His wife Paula was just three months pregnant with their daughter Kerri when Rader was killing his seventh victim.

While his kids grew up and he taught them right from wrong, he killed three more victims. It is even possible that on the day his daughter got married he was planning his attack on yet another.

Many people found themselves asking, "How didn't we know?" Even his wife whom he had been married to for 34 years and slept in the same bed with him had no idea that he was a murderer.

Rader was a father who taught his children how to camp, fish, and garden. He took his family on vacations, did not allow swearing and was a great Boy Scout leader. His children referred to him as the perfect father.

Dennis Rader was a wolf in sheep's clothing. He was the exception to the rule. Most serial killers are loners, they are deranged, and however, Rader is not any of that.

Nor was Robert Yates who killed 15 and had been married with five children. Everyone described him as a generous man as well as a dedicated father.

Gary Ridgway took the lives of at least 49 women all while being the perfect father.

It is people like Rader, Yates, and Ridgway that are the most terrifying of all. They are the people that live next door. They are the people who are in charge of the clubs that our children attend. They are leaders in our churches.

They are the people that we look at and think they have the world by the horns. They are also the people that show us that it is not only psychopaths, sociopaths, schizophrenics, or other mentally ill people that commit murder but that anyone… Even the guy that lives across the street and looks like the perfect father can be a serial killer. Would you even know?

If these men's own families had no idea that the men that they loved and that had raised them were committing heinous crimes how do you think you could figure it out?

Is There A Pattern?

We once thought that we had enough serial killers to determine that there was a pattern, that maybe we would be able to determine who would become a serial killer. Sadly that is not the case.

However, there are a few interesting similarities among serial killers.

Serial killers do not generally attack people that they know. Instead, they tend to target only strangers, meaning that if there is a serial killer on the loose, it is anyone's guess that he will target.

To a person who has not studied the minds of serial killers, it may seem that the locations or the victims that they choose are random; however, there is a pattern to that as well.

For example, if we look at Garavito, we know that he had a pattern of choosing boys between the ages of 6 and 16, the same age which he was sexually abused. Some serial killers will target prostitutes because they are easy prey. Others might go after the woman walking down the alley alone at night.

What do they all have in common? They are easily overpowered and cannot fight their attacker off most of the time.

The scary part is not when someone like Garavito is captured. While his crimes are horrific, there was nothing spectacular about him except for the fact that he was able to get away with the crime for such a long period of time. However, we already know that this was because so many children go missing in Colombia on a daily basis that the police simply do not investigate instances of poor missing children… That is until they turn up in mass graves.

What is terrifying is when it is someone that is well respected in the community. When it is someone that everyone liked. Maybe someone that you would let into your home. Or perhaps someone that you let takes your children camping.

It is most terrifying when it is found that someone who is just like the rest of us has gone on a killing spree and no one ever suspected it.

I believe that it is important for us to continue research as it pertains to murderers and to serial killers. We as a society need to understand what has made these people snap.

Is it a mental illness? Is it caused by trauma in their lives? Was it the result of abuse as a child? Perhaps it was caused by some type of head trauma? Is it possible that one day they just snapped?

Of course, we already have the profiles of serial killers. For example, white men who commit serial killings are often single, suffer from bipolar disorder, and are between the ages of 25 and 40.

However, there are many serial killers as mentioned above that simply do not fit this profile.

We learned how many serial killers come from families or homes where they suffered from abuse as children. However, not everyone who suffers from abuse becomes a killer and not everyone who becomes a killer suffered from abuse.

Mass murderers are often very intelligent, however, when they begin killing there is no planning.

Yet there are those murderers who get some sick pleasure from planning the murders. Most often it begins with fantasizing about killing a person. They will think about what they would do, however, when this no longer satisfies them, they have to act out their fantasies, much like a pedophile.

Many times, it is found that a serial killer simply desired attention, that they were lonely, or that they wanted fame.

Of course, then we have those who are angry with someone at work or at school such as what happened at Columbine. These people go on a killing rampage simply out of anger.

Of course, there are people out there who want to become as famous as Ted Bundy, The Zodiac, Holmes, Eric Harris and Dylan Klebold, Charles Manson, or Jeffrey Dahmer.

Why? Because they will forever be remembered. They want to feel that they have some worth, some value, or that they have done something with their lives.

They want to be remembered because as long as humans exist on this planet, there are going to be those out there who are fascinated if not obsessed with learning as much as they can about serial killers.

The problem, however, that this leaves us with is that no matter how hard we try, no matter how many categories we create and no matter how many tests that we do, we are never going to understand what is going on inside of the mind of a killer.

Why? There are simply too many variables. If there was only one type of serial killer, or all serial killers committed murder for the same reason, maybe we could begin to understand what was or is going on in their heads, however, there simply are too many reasons.

Sadly, we also have to understand that as we are reading this book, there could be another serial killer on the loose. How long will it be before we find out that another serial killer murdered hundreds of people and somehow went undetected?

There are so many vulnerable groups in our world today. Oddly enough in a world where you would not think that people could go missing without being noticed, it continues to happen every single day.

Who will be the next Garavito? Who will the victims be? Who will be the next Night Stalker? The next Zodiac? Charles Manson or Ted Bundy?

Most of us would like to think that the days of serial killing are far behind us but I believe that Garavito showed us that this is not the case. He was captured only 18 years ago. The majority of those boys that he killed would not even be 30 years old if he had not killed them.

They would be husbands and fathers. Their families would have been saved so much suffering.

So what do we do with the serial killer? Do we lock them up in prison for the rest of their life as we have in the past? Do we kill them, taking their life for the lives that they have taken?

Or do we try to find out what is wrong with them and try to fix them? Maybe by finding out what is wrong with them, we can predict who is most likely to become a serial killer in the future and treat them before they commit a crime?

Personally, I believe that anything is possible. However, I also believe that we need to do the thing that is going to prevent more victims in the future. As for Garavito, The Beast, murderer, and torturer of over 300 young boys, I do not think that the people of Colombia will be letting him walk out of that prison anytime soon. And if the government fails the people, allowing Garavito out of that prison on anything but a gurney, I believe that the people of Colombia will ensure that justice is served. For every single little life that was taken.

It is those lives that we must not forget were taken. While men like Garavito are interesting to study, we must not forget that he was a monster. He tortured, raped, and killed 300 young boys who had their entire lives ahead of them. Why should he have any life ahead of him?

Made in the USA
Las Vegas, NV
23 May 2024

90244192R00069